Compact Cymru

Stone Quarries and Mineral Mines in Llŷn

Des Marshall

Gwasg Carreg Gwalch

First published in 2023

ISBN: 978-1-84524-522-1
Cover design: Eleri Owen
Map on page 9 by Alison Davies Mapping Co. Ltd.

Published by Gwasg Carreg Gwalch,
12 Iard yr Orsaf, Llanrwst, Wales LL26 0EH
tel: 01492 642031
email: books@carreg-gwalch.cymru
website: www.carreg-gwalch.cymru

The uppermost drum house and drum skeleton at Nant Gadwen

Contents

Introduction

Llŷn (to outsiders) is usually regarded as being west of a line drawn from Caernarfon to Porthmadog. However, the true Llŷn is to the west of a line drawn from Trefor to Pwllheli. It is the latter distinction used within these pages, widened slightly to stretch from Clynnog-fawr to Cricieth. The peninsula is a long, often wild and wonderful finger of land stretching some 30 miles into the Irish Sea marking the northern boundary of Bae Ceredigion (*Cardigan Bay*). For much of its length the width is only 8 miles and has sea on three sides. There are many secret coves which, years ago, were ideal for another 'industry', smuggling. The aim of this book is to highlight the wealth of industry once carried out.

Associated with the peninsula is the island of Ynys Enlli (*Bardsey Island*) lying two miles offshore. There is evidence to suggest that Neolithic people lived here. (The Neolithic period can be regarded as being 4,300 B.C to 2,000 B.C.). In the 5th century it was a sanctuary for persecuted Christians. Ynys Enlli was visited by St Gadfan in 516 and built St Mary's Abbey. St Cadfan was the first abbot between 516 and 542. Three pilgrimages here were equivalent of one to Rome. It is rumoured that 20,000 saints are buried here. Perhaps it was because monks who retreated to the island towards the end of their lives were thought to be saints and ended up dying there.

In years gone by Llŷn was a noisy busy and industrial area with large stone quarries starting to make huge scars on the mountainsides. Today, the peninsula is a quiet pastoral area with small houses, cottages and farms. Many of the villages were built from the local stone as is evident from the many stone quarries both large and small. Other industries developed as the years passed with mineral mining being undertaken. Mining for Manganese, was perhaps, the largest industry after stone quarrying. The two areas where this was mined were from above Porth Ysgo in the Nant y Gadwen and at Rhiw between 1894 and 1945.

Curling stones used in the 2002 Salt Lake City and 2006 Turin winter Olympics came from the rock in the quarry above Trefor. This special granitic rock, microgranodiorite, is only found in two places in the whole world. One is found in the Firth of Clyde, Ailsa Craig and the other, the quarry above Trefor. The Ailsa Craig source has run out of rock leaving Trefor as the only place left. Blue hone and common green rock were both found on Ailsa Craig. It has low water absorption preventing the action of repeatedly freezing water from eroding it. Trefor has blue, grey and pink rock. Experiments on rock from other areas are under way to find a suitable alternative such as western Canada and a more suitable one in India as this bears similar qualities to the rock at Trefor.

Many areas on Llŷn quarried stone with the main area being above Trefor and Nant Gwrtheyrn. Quarrying began in earnest as 'setts' were made to pave city streets. At one time and, perhaps, due to the quarries Porthdinllaen close to Nefyn was promoted to be the main port for shipping to Ireland. Sadly this did not happen as Holyhead was favoured for this. Stone was shipped out from Trefor and Nant Gwrtheyrn. As the quarry above Trefor grew so did the village with the harbour and pier being built for exporting setts. Other areas where stone was quarried were Mynydd Tir y Cwmwd at Llanbedrog, Trwyn Dwmi at Porth Pistyll and Carreg yr Imbill (Gimlet Rock) in Pwllheli. There were several quarries close to Nefyn. Gwylwyr for instance had its own incline that was used to take stone to the quarry's jetty at Wern beach. Another was on Mynydd Nefyn and called John Lloyd. Close to Pistyll were the quarries of Tŷ Mawr, Bodeilas and Tŷ Gwyn. The word *Chwarel* is Welsh for quarry and is usually used to prefix the quarry name as in Chwarel Porth y Nant! The earliest stone production was the stone axe factory dating back 5 – 6,000 years in the Neolithic Age on the north eastern side of Mynydd Rhiw.

Quarry workers had an extremely hard life. Often they walked many miles to work in the morning and after grafting all day had to walk back. One description notes that workers were often bent double in the teeth of a howling gale. To earn an income they became tied to quarrying the rock. In fact the author and publisher Myrddin ap Dafydd wrote – *coming to work they were bent double in the teeth of the wind. They are tied to earning their living from this rock, as if they chiselled it with their fingernails, summer or winter, it's the same yoke of stone on their shoulders. But they, on the path in the sky, bending, stumbling to the top of the mountain, they are the cornerstones of our walls – and we, so far from the wind that cuts like a knife, are shaped from what they once were.*

Lead was mined close to Abersoch at Penrhyn Du and was established in 1638. It is possible that the Romans were first to exploit and mine lead here. With the mine being close to a headland it was easy to load the ore onto ships. The main surviving relic here is the fine engine house. There were also lead mines around Llanengan with the stark remains of a tall chimney. This was part of the Porth Neigwl mine. Whether the purpose of the chimney was for ventilation or to act as a flue for the beam engine below is uncertain. It has been reported that coal was found and mined on the land of Brynhunog Fawr in 1837 and at Rhos Cabli in 1844. There was enough support and evidence that 'The Rhoshirwaun Coal and Mining Company' was formed.

Barytes was quarried and mined close to Aberdaron. Although not in operation long 1905 – 1913 it was briefly worked again in 1918. However, it was certainly worked before those dates. Jasper was quarried on Mynydd Carreg. This can be accessed from the coastal path and is close to one of, if not the best, beach on the Llŷn, Whistling Sands. So called because the sand 'sings' or 'whistles' when wet feet walk over the dry sand.

Geology of the Llŷn is quite complex. The majority of the peninsula is formed from volcanic activity from the Ordovician Age, part of the Palaeozoic Era that lasted from circa 541 to 252 million years ago. (The term Ordovician is derived from a tribe of fierce people called the Ordovices). Rocks from the Cambrian Age occur south of Abersoch. There are intrusions of rhyolite and granite like rock composed of porphyrite and quartz. Igneous rock from the Ordovician Age formed the hills such as Yr Eifl. Gabbro is found at the western end of Porth Neigwl (Hell's Mouth). The rock in the north-west part of the Llŷn, to the west of a line drawn from Nefyn to Aberdaron, dates to the Precambrian Era further back in the mists of time prior to 541 million years ago. Boulder clay was left in a number of places after the last Ice Age, notably at Porthdinllaen where it was used to manufacture bricks in the 18th and 19th centuries.

Tourism is now the main industry with

the honey pots of Abersoch and Aberdaron at one time a hive of noisy industry now ringing to the sound of cars and people. Pwllheli is regarded as the 'capital'. It too sees many visitors. Now being well supplied with holiday accommodation it is easy to explore Pen Llŷn. The best maps to use are the Ordnance Survey Explorer 1:25,000 series 253 Lleyn Peninsula West/Pen Llŷn Ardal Orllewinol and 254 Lleyn Peninsula East/Pen Llŷn Ardal Ddwyreiniol. They give much more detail than the 1:50,000 series.

It is VERY important to remember that quarries and mines can be extremely dangerous places. DO NOT venture into any of the manganese mines. There are many hazards that include deep shafts. slippery slopes, old mining rubbish and rock falls being encountered. Walks along the coastal path need care in many places as there are some long drops into the sea.

My reason for writing this book is to record what little is left of the infrastructure of these ancient sites. Quarries add to the drama of the area, especially the ones above Trefor on Garn For. As with the slate books I have photographed these remains as nature, vandals and souvenir hunters will soon leave the area devoid of these structures. If visiting please remember the saying, '*take nothing but pictures and leave nothing other than footprints*'. So PLEASE take all your litter home with you. A can of pop is much heavier when you bring it from home and is much lighter when its contents have been consumed. As too are plastic bottles. Please also remember to take wrappings, plastic bags and fruit peel home too. Above all please adhere to the country code as follows:

The Country Code

Respect other people.
Consider the local community and other people enjoying the outdoors.
Park carefully so access to gateways and driveways are clear.
Leave gates and property as you find them.
Follow paths but give way to others where it's narrow.
Protect the natural environment.
Leave no trace of your visit, take ALL your litter home.
Be careful with BBQs, avoid using single use barbecues and don't light fires. Single use barbecues are a major source of wild fires being started.
Keep dogs under effective control.

Dog poo – bag it and bin it, or take it with you. DO NOT leave it by the side of the path or adorning a wayside tree to be picked up later as this rarely happens.
Enjoy the outdoors.
Plan ahead, check what facilities are open, be prepared.
Follow advice and local signs.

1 Mynydd Rhiw stone axe factory
2 Tyddyn Hywel stone quarry
3 Tan y Graig stone quarry
4 Trefor stone quarry
5 Cae'r Nant stone quarry
6 Porth y Nant stone quarry
7 Carreg y Llam stone quarry
8 Gwylwyr stone quarry
9 Mynydd Tir y Cwmwd stone quarry
10 Trwyn Dwmi stone quarry
11 Nant Gadwen manganese mine
12 Rhiw/Benallt manganese mines
13 Penrhyn Du lead/copper mine
14 Porth Neigwl lead mine
15 Mynydd Carreg jasper quarry
16 Gwaith y Pompren barytes quarry

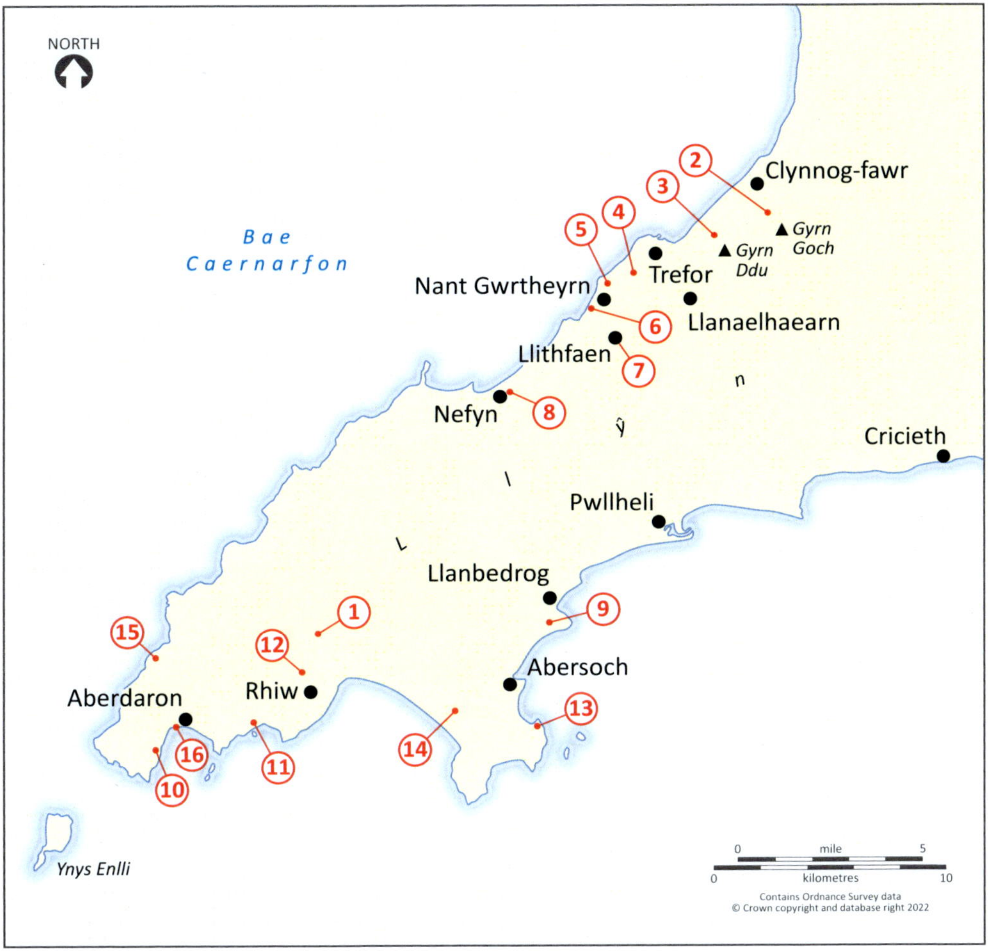
NORTH
Bae Caernarfon
Clynnog-fawr
Gyrn Goch
Gyrn Ddu
Trefor
Nant Gwrtheyrn
Llanaelhaearn
Llithfaen
Nefyn
Cricieth
Pwllheli
Llanbedrog
Abersoch
Rhiw
Aberdaron
Ynys Enlli
1
2
3
4
5
6
7
8
9
10
11
12
13
14
15
16
0 mile 5
0 kilometres 10
Contains Ordnance Survey data
© Crown copyright and database right 2022

Section 1 – Stone Quarries

Overview

Although often called granite the rock is actually a microgranodiorite, a medium grained igneous rock. with grains between 1 and 5mm. It is a mix of two related types of rock, granite and diorite. The gran root comes from the Latin *granum* meaning grain. Simply put, micro = small, gran = grain and diorite or small grained diorite. Diorite is an intrusive igneous rock and is a composition between low-silica gabbro and high-silica granite. Granite consists mainly of potassium feldspars with a low percentage of dark iron and magnesium minerals whereas granodiorite contains more calcium and sodium.

Granite minerals composing the rock are mostly quartz and feldspar have a low thermal conductivity. A too hot or too cool a surface will negatively affect the thin film of water on which a curling stone glides. Granite is also very resistant to erosion and weathering maintaining its properties over time. Granodiorite has greater than 20% of quartz and between 65% and 90% feldspar. It also has a high sodium and calcium content. Granodiorite is usually only exposed on the surface after uplift and erosion have taken place.

Stone quarrying became the largest industry on Pen Llŷn due to the demand for 'setts' to pave the streets in England. Quarries were worked between 1830 until 1962 and very spasmodically since. The quarries provided much work for the men in the area especially the main ones developed above Trefor and around Nant Gwrtheyrn. There is evidence that the earliest industrial production dates from the Neolithic Age, some five to six thousand years ago, at the stone axe factory on Mynydd Rhiw. Sadly there is not much to see there today.

Stone quarries had developed at Penmaenmawr. These also provided setts to pave English streets. People would move between these two areas. Quarrymen also moved from England, especially Cornwall, to the area.

A sett is also known as a Block or Belgian Block. They are generally rectangular in shape and were in general use to pave streets, especially steeper ones, until tarmac became popular with the advent of motorised vehicles. Setts gave horses hooves better grip than a smooth surface. Setts are often incorrectly called ‘cobblestones’. Whereas setts are crafted by man from a block of granite a cobblestone is a naturally rounded rock.

As well as being quarried predominantly for setts some of the stone was for use of lump or building stone as well as for hand broken macadam stone for road building as well as for railway ballast. Huge stone crushing machines were installed such as Carreg y Llam for large scale production of road stone, railway ballast and concrete aggregate.

The main stone quarries of Pen Llŷn are:

Tyddyn Hywel – SH 398 471
Tan y Graig – SH 390 466
Trefor – SH 363 460
Carreg y Llam – SH 337 438
Cae’r Nant – SH 354 453
Porth y Nant – SH 335 438
Gwylwyr – SH 319 414
Carreg y Imbill (Gimlet Rock) – SH 386 342
Mynydd Tir y Cwmwd – SH 328 304
Trwyn Dwmi (Porth y Pistyll) – SH 163 251
Stone Axe factory, Mynydd Rhiw – SH 233 295 and SH 233 299

Minor quarries around Nefyn were Tŷ Mawr/Bodeilas SH 320 416, Moel Tŷ Gwyn SH 329 415, Moel Dywyrch SH 324 407 and John Lloyd SH 314 407.

Stone Axe Factory – Mynydd Rhiw

Map: Ordnance Survey 1:25,000 Lleyn Peninsula West/Pen Llŷn Ardal Orllewinol
Grid reference: SH 233 299

Situated to the south west of the Peninsula above the tiny village of Rhiw is Mynydd Rhiw. At 304 metres it is the highest summit hereabouts. The hill comprises ridges of hard volcanic rock interspersed by a finer grained shale type of rock which were exploited during the Neolithic period, the final division of the Stone Age also called the New Stone Age. It was here that stone tools, such as axes, knives and scrapers were manufactured.

The site at SH 233 299 was the first to be discovered in the late 1950's when fieldwork discovered three hollows. These were initially thought to be round houses. Closer examination revealed that the

hollows were composed of debris from stone axe manufacture and were the remains of five quarry pits with a maximum diameter of 15 metres. Sadly the remains are largely obscured by gorse and heather but can just be made out.

A later field work in 2005 discovered another site at SH 233 295. Here hollows were found over a 600 metres long length of the hillside. These indicated that the Neolithic people were capable of digging some 2 metres down to extract loose stone rather than quarrying the bedrock. Radiocarbon dating suggests this was in the period 3,650 B.C. to 3,050 B.C. The stone dug out was most likely used locally rather than moved out of the area, possibly for cairn building or agricultural purposes.

1. Looking across to Garn Fadryn from the site of the stone axe factory on Mynydd Rhiw; 2. One of the slight remains of the stone axe factory on Mynydd Rhiw

Tyddyn Hywel

Map: Ordnance Survey 1:25,000 Lleyn Peninsula East/Pen Llŷn Ardal Ddwyreiniol Grid reference: SH 398 471

This stone quarry is easily seen from the A499 road. Coming from Caernarfon it is situated between the tiny village of Gyrn Goch and the turn off to Trefor. The approach from SH 394 475 into the quarry is arduous to say the least. Before the really tortuous bit there is a wonderful zigzag line of steps up the boulder slope before the tortuous ascent over scree. Other remains include a short but degraded incline, drum house with decaying drum and ruined buildings. The steps are, however, a fine feature and easy to reach. There is not much of note on the quarry floor. In 1910 this quarry was being worked by the British Grey Granite Co (Kidderminster). Subsequently in the 1930's this and Tan y Graig were operated by the Thomas W Ward group and eventually by RMC. The quarry workers struggled to develop manageable faces. As such they became inactive after 1949. The only activity seen nowadays are infrequent visits by rock climbers for a very out of the way experience.

1. The degraded incline and cable at Tyddyn Hywel stone quarry; 2. The start of a remarkable series of steps climbing the huge boulder field leading to the quarry; 3. The steps higher up the boulder field below the quarry; 4. The drum house ruin at the top of the incline at Tyddyn Hywel stone quarry; 5. Looking down to the drum house and ruined buildings

2

3

4

5

Tan y Graig

***Map:* Ordnance Survey 1:25,000 Lleyn Peninsula East/Pen Llŷn Ardal Ddwyreiniol**
***Grid reference:* SH 390 466**

Like Tyddyn Hywel this quarry is easily seen from the A499 road close to the turn off to Trefor when approaching from Caernarfon. Turning off the A499 to the left leads to Seaview Terrace, the Tan y Graig houses. A signed path starting from SH 385 467, just past these, leads up towards Rock Cottage and thence on a clear signed track to the quarry.

Tan y Graig opened in 1864 for making setts. Several attempts by different companies saw the quarry eventually amalgamate with the nearby Tyddyn Hywel stone quarry which was owned by Enderby & Stoney Stanton Granite Co Ltd in 1916. At this time they produced stone chippings for use with tarmac rather than setts. The paving of streets with setts was being phased out in favour of tar surfaced roads. The chippings were moved from the quarry on a two feet gauge railway to the pier at Bryn yr Eryr for exportation.

In 1918 this was replaced by the Enderby (Welsh) Granite Co Ltd. In 1928 the company was wound up by a Sheffield company, Thomas W Ward Ltd who then took over operations in 1930. They continued quarrying until 1947.

Just like Tyddyn Hywel the only activity seen here nowadays are infrequent visits by rock climbers for a very out of the way experience.

1. Tan y Graig stone quarry on Gyrn Ddu when viewed from the A499 close to the road junction to Trefor;
2. General view looking up to Tan y Graig stone quarry;
3. Looking down onto the incline;
4. Ruined waliau where the setts were once made

1

2

3

2

3

4

1. The main Tan y Graig stone quarry;
2. Looking down on the ruins from the upper level;
3. Waliau where the setts were made at Tan y Graig;
4. A huge fireplace in one of the ruined buildings;
5. Tan y Graig seen from the walk up with the incline to the right

Trefor

***Map:** Ordnance Survey 1:25,000 Lleyn Peninsula East/Pen Llŷn Ardal Ddwyreiniol*
***Grid reference:** SH 363 458*

Sometimes referred to as Eifl Quarry, it was the largest stone quarry on Pen Llŷn. Locally the quarry was known as Y Gwaith Mor or simply just Y Gwaith. Oddly Trefor was spelt Trevor and still appearing as such as late as 1903 on the 1:63,360 OS map. There is no V in the Welsh language nowadays. F is pronounced as V. Geologically speaking Trefor Granite is referred to as the *Garnfor Multiple Intrusions*. It is termed thus as it composed of several different granitic types of rock that are found in the quarry. Three of which can be identified. These are referred to by the quarrymen as pink, blue and grey granite. All these can be used for curling stones. Pink granite forms the core of the intrusion especially at the top of the quarry. Blue granite forms the margins of the overall structure and where pink and blue meet the difference is quite distinct. The granite is around 450 million years old and was formed when Wales was a volcanic area similar to island groups such as groups found in the Pacific, Japan or even the Aleutian Islands. All these are situated above subduction zones. (*A subduction zone is a collision between two tectonic plates. One of these sinks into the mantle beneath the other. One example of this is where an oceanic plate descends beneath another oceanic plate; for example Japan, Indonesia and the Aleutian Islands or two,*

1

2

alternatively, where an oceanic plate descends beneath a continental plate. For example South and Central America and the Cascade Volcanoes on the Pacific Coast of Washington and Oregon).

The remnants of the Welsh volcanoes and their deposits now form the rocky and craggy Snowdonia. However, the magma that does not reach the surface will, in time, slowly cool and crystallise. This then produces medium to coarse grained igneous rock such as the granites. The Trefor granite and other associated granites of the area form the prominent hills of Pen Llŷn and is characteristic of this process. Trefor granite is no longer in the pristine state it was when it first crystallised. A subsequent, but mild, metamorphic change resulted in the rock becoming slightly hydrated. The pink, white and the opaqueness of the feldspars in the granite occurred due to a reaction with hot water to form a veneer of hydrated minerals on the surfaces of the crystals as well as the surfaces of micropores within them. Even the iron magnesium silicates were hydrated so that of all the common minerals found in granite it is only quartz that has remained totally unaltered. The blue, also known as blue hone has very low water absorption

1. General view of Trefor stone quarry from the road leading into the village from the north; 2. Looking up to the remains of the main quarry buildings from the access road. Garn For is in the background;
3. Immaculate stone walling on one of the internal incline walls; 4. The entrance into the lowest quarry

1

2

3

which prevents it from repeatedly freezing and thus eroding the stone.

Fortunately, however, even though the rock does not polish as well as unaltered granite it still retained its high resistance to crushing making it an ideal and necessary requirement for curling stones. Because of this 'accident' of geological history this unique Welsh rock is still sought after for the manufacture of curling stones. Curling Stones from Trefor were used most recently at the Winter Olympic Games in the ones held in at the 2002 Salt Lake City games and 2006 when they were held in Turin.

A note here about Curling Stones. Ailsa Craig a small rocky island over 300 metres high in the middle of the Firth of Clyde, Scotland, has been the traditional source for the rock to make curling stones where Blue Hone and Ailsa Craig Common Green were quarried. Blue Hone has a very low water absorption rate preventing freezing water eroding the stone. Ailsa Craig Common Green is of lesser quality. The island is now a nature reserve having environmental issues in place which include the prohibition of blasting.

1. Trefor from the lowest level; 2. Shot holes; 3. A feral goat, one of the quarry's residents

Trefor granite comes in shades of pink, blue, and grey and supplies curling stone rock. The granite blocks are sold to Kays Crafts Curling Workshop, Mauchline in Ayrshire, Scotland as well as to the Canada Curling Stone Company in Ontario for shaping and polishing. Kays have been making curling stones since 1851. They have the exclusive rights to the Ailsa Craig granite. These were granted by the Marquess of Ailsa, whose family has owned the island since 1560.

Curling Stones are shaped and smoothed into a circular shape with a concave top and bottom. Curling Stones must weigh between 38 and 46 pounds (17.24 and 19.96 kgs). A handle is attached to the top of the stone. The stone must not exceed a maximum circumference of 36 inches (914.4mm) and a minimum height of 4.5 inches (114.3mm). The only part of the stone in contact with the ice is known as the running surface. This is a narrow, flat ring ¼ to ½ inch (6.4 to 12.7mm) wide and about 5 inches (130mm) in diameter. The sides of the stone are convex in shape down to the ring. The inside of the ring is hollowed out concave to allow clearance with the ice. This idea was first conceived

1. & 2. Remains of the main works; 3. Fine stone wall on the level up from the main buildings

and proposed by J S Russell of Toronto, Ontario, Canada sometime around 1870 subsequently adopted by Andrew Kay of Kays Crafts. Finally, it has been said that the stone from Trefor is superior to the rock on Ailsa Craig?

Trefor stone quarry was established in 1830 by Samuel Holland (his father was a pioneer for the Ffestiniog Railway). When Trevor Jones became quarry supervisor the village at the foot took his name. A Welsh poet, Eben Fardd, wrote in strict Englyn metre praising the new quarry owners, Hutton and Roscoe. (An Englyn, or plural englynion, is a traditional Welsh and Cornish short poem. It uses quantative metres involving the counting of syllables and rigid patterns of rhyme and half rhyme. Each line contains a repeating pattern of consonants and accent known as cynghanedd).

By 1850 the quarries were owned by the Welsh Granite Co. Ltd. In 1911 the Penmaenmawr and Llanfairfechan quarries amalgamated with the Trefor ones to form the Penmaenmawr and Welsh Granite Co. Ltd. By 1931 Trefor quarry had produced 1,157,000 tons of setts. There are nine distinct levels rising some 305 metres from the lowest one. After setts were no longer needed the quarry started producing chippings and stone for monumental work. Once quarried and on the quarry floor the stone was split in a remarkable way using a system of plugs and wedges. A series of 4 inch (100mm) holes were drilled into which the plugs and wedges were driven by a sledge hammer. Apparently the stone

1. An internal view of the old buildings; 2. Waliau used for sett making; 3. Waliau with Gyrn Goch on the left and Gyrn Ddu on the right

split 'as cleanly and sweetly as if cut with a knife'. The stone was brought down in larger pieces more so than at the quarries at Penmaenmawr.

The infrastructure was great with rail served levels, workshops, inclines, magazine, bins, crusher house and a fine 3,018 feet (920 metres) long incline with a 1 foot 11 inches (600mm) gauge tramway at 1:75 which continued on the level past further offices and through the village (this had a siding) to terminate at the pier. The main cargo was for setts that were being shipped to Liverpool and other cities for paving. The lower section of the incline was worked with a steam locomotive.

At one time all the stone crushed at Trefor was cut by hand to a size that could be dealt with. Initially this was done with a 30 inch (750mm) x 18 inch (450mm) jaw crusher. The product was then transported by wagons to the crushing mill down a number of steep inclines. Later a 48 inch (1200mm) x 36 inch (900mm) jaw crusher was installed on the fifth level. After passing through the main crusher the stone travelled down using gravity to the level above the crushing mill and transported there in train loads. This saves money down steep inclines that wre used only to bring down sawn slabs and blocks to the stone factory on the lowest level.

The factory housed carborundum saws, polishing machines and a sand blasting plant. Adjacent to the factory were the stone masons' sheds. many activities took place that were a tribute to the craftsmanship, accuracy of eye and dexterity of hand. Compressed air was laid on in later years for the pneumatic tools used by the masons who in addition to the architectural and monumental work produced curling stones. Inevitably, closure came in 1963.

The village developed quickly after the quarry opened with Doc Bach, quay and harbour built for exporting setts. The harbour was opened by Samuel Holland. It was presumed at this time that the harbour of Porthdinllaen would become the major port of the area for ferries to Ireland. This did not happen as Holyhead became the main port instead. Stone was carried in railway wagons to the harbour using a cable operated incline for the controlled descent.

There was as a stocking area near to the loading quay that stored stone of different sizes. When required for shipment the stone chippings were loaded by a 'half yard' shovel to quarry trucks which were then either tipped directly to the ship or to a conveyor feeding the 3,000 ton capacity concrete hopper. Ships of 1,200 tons could dock here. On the seaward side of the breakwater, seen today, was the wooden jetty. Sadly this disappeared in 2017 after storm Ophelia.

1

2

3

1. Remains of the main works;
2. Internal view into the main building;
3. Remains of the main works but note the fine stone walling;
4. An internal tramway with wooden sleepers still in situ;
5. General view of the buildings and walls looking up from the lowest level;
6. Nefyn Pier in 2022. Note that the wooden part has disappeared;
7. Trefor pier seen from Tan y Graig in February 2022;
8. Looking towards the pier at Trefor from the lower slopes of Gyrn Goch in March 2016

1

2

3

1. Looking towards the pier at Trefor from the lower slopes of Gyrn Goch with the shadowy from of Trefor looming to the left in March 2016;
2. West End Cottages close to Trefor with Trefor Quarry rearing up in the background;
3. Looking up to Trefor Quarry on Garn Fôr;
4. View down to Trefor from the summit of Garn Fôr. To the right is Gyrn Goch and Gyrn Ddu;
5. View of Trefor from Garn Fôr;
6. Looking across to the stone quarry on Garn Fôr from Garn Ganol (Yr Eifl);
7. Remnants of very old stone quarrying (excavation) on Garn Ganol overlooking Bwlch yr Eifl facing Garn Fôr

The Stone Quarries associated with Nant Gwrtheyrn

The wonderful and isolated village of Nant Gwrtheyrn, originally Porth y Nant, was built during the second half of the 19th century to house the quarry workers of the booming stone industry. Before quarrying commenced in 1851 there were perhaps only three farms in the valley with 16 people living in seclusion. In 1861 a Liverpool company, Kneeshaw and Lupton, bought Nant Gwrtheyrn and built twenty six new houses for the influx of quarry workers who travelled from far and wide. As such the village thrived. By 1900 there were around 2,000 quarrymen along a five mile stretch of coastline from Tan y Graig to Pistyll.

In 1878 two terraces of houses were built at right angles to each other as more quarry workers came to the area. One was named Sea View as it faced the sea and the other Mountain View as it looked towards the quarry. Quarrymen were joined by their wives and children. In 1875 Capel Seilo was built for the ever increasing population of Calvinistic Methodists who now lived in the area. In 1883 the Plas was built. This was a very fine detached house for the quarry manager to the west of Mountain View.

A jetty was built below Porth y Nant so that ships could transport the setts to Liverpool and onwards to Manchester and Birkenhead. In 1886 the census indicated that the number of people living in Nant Gwrtheyrn was 200. Jetties were also built below Cae'r Nant and Carreg y Llam. At that time some 150 to 200 ships landed each week. Whilst they took setts out they brought in coal, wood and foodstuffs amongst other much needed items. Women, if they were lucky, managed to get free trips to Liverpool when they brought back fancy goods and decorations. Now with a chapel, its own shops, school and of course house the village was booming. In 1910 the local council decided to change the name back from Porth y Nant to Nant Gwrtheyrn.

The Welsh poem at the memorial translates into English as:

On their knees, who are they
That come to work through the teeth of the wind?
Men tied to the bread of this rock
With their nails chiselled to it
Summer or Winter, the same yoke
Of stones on their shoulders
But they, on this celestial path
Bent, tripping to the peak
Of the mountain, they are the cornerstones
Of our walls – and us,
So far from the knife of the winds
Are the shavings of what they were.

In 1911 the quarries centred on Nant Gwrtheyrn merged with other local quarries to form the Welsh Granite Company. They were managed by the Darbyshire family. A unique and multicultural community developed as the

1. The sculpture, erected as a memorial to the quarrymen, at the car park before the road descends into Nant Gwrtheyrn;
2. One of the Celtic carvings

families coming to Nant were from England, Scotland as well of course from Wales itself. The quarry manager lived in the house to the left of Capel Seilo which was also the village school.

When tarmac became the first choice for road building demand for stone marked the decline of the village in the 1930's. The population fell dramatically with the result that the shops closed and fell vacant, the school also closed as well as the chapel. Stone quarrying was virtually abandoned mid-way during the Second World War. The villagers dispersed with the last people moving away in 1959. The cottages then started to fall into disrepair. During the 1970's the village was 'discovered' by the New Atlantis Commune of hippies. They lived very roughly as there was no sewage, electricity or even water. As such much damage was caused. The group burnt the floors, doors and anything else they could find. Also they covered the walls with graffiti. The jetties collapsed in the 1970's.

In 1978 the whole village was in ruins but it was bought by a charitable trust, *Ymddiriedolaeth Nant Gwrtheyrn* who began restoring the houses and Nant is now the Welsh National Language Centre. Gwrtheyrn translates to Vortigern but 'King Vortigern' probably never visited here although he was in Snowdonia. There are many legends associated with village, 'The Three Curses', 'Elis Bach', 'The German Spy', 'The Eagle and the Baby', 'Luned Bengoch' and, perhaps, the most famous one of all, 'Rhys a Meinir'. All these and the story of 'Nant' can be found in an excellent book written by Dr Carl Clowes entitled Nant Gwrtheyrn obtainable from the shop or café.

Briefly a résumé of a few of these is:

Vortigern was a 5th century British ruler who attempted to negotiate with invading Saxons. He failed and was forced to flee to eventually find sanctuary in the valley. Gwrtheyrn is the Welsh form of Vortigern.

1. The sculpture, erected as a memorial to the quarrymen, at the car park before the road descends into Nant Gwrtheyrn. Garn Ganol the highest peak in Llŷn is to the left; 2. Setts loaded into a tram at Nant Gwrtheyrn; 3. Setts; 4. An artists' impression of how Porth y Nant might have looked. This can be seen at Nant Gwrtheyrn; 5. Several of the goats to be found at Nant Gwrtheyrn

Rhys and Meinir were two cousins who fell in love with each other. They had arranged to be married at the church in Clynnog Fawr. When the wedding day arrived Meinir failed to turn up. Rhys was grief stricken and he spent months searching for Meinir until a lightning strike split open a hollow tree. Inside he saw the skeleton of Meinir still in her wedding dress.

Elis Bach lived in Tŷ Canol in the early part of the 19th century. He was not a tall man, his legs were only 30 centimetres long, he was, however, the fastest runner and was given the job of rounding up the mountain sheep and goats ready for the Nant market. One day two strangers arrived and offered well over the going price for many of their purchases. The men were subsequently invited to Elis' home to enjoy some home cooked food.

Somewhat taken aback by their behaviour Elis hid in a cupboard where he overheard their plan to steal the sheep. When the strangers left after paying a small amount just for the food, they scurried back up the 'corkscrew' road with the stolen sheep. Elis raced after them on a different pach along with his faithful dog, Meg to cut them off.

Getting in front of them Elis lay in wait at a bend in the road leaping out when these men passed. Startled and alarmed the men fled towards Pistyll while Elis and Meg took the sheep back into Nant.

The German Spy. During World War II a mysterious stranger arrived and moved into a remote, solitary bungalow above Carreg y Llam. Her name was Margaret Gladys Fisher. Her odd behaviour brought her to the attention of the local people who started to think she was a spy. They believed rightly or wrongly that she signalled to German boats or submarines in the bay below. In the early hours one morning in 1943 her bungalow was found to be burnt to the ground. As such it will never be known whether she was a spy or not! Her dogs did not bark and no-one could identify the charred remains. It was presumed that Margaret had staged her death and escaped to Germany on a boat that came in on a favourable tide.

The Three Monks. Three Monks arrived in Nant shortly after Gwrtheryn's death. They were on their way to Ynys Enlli (Bardsea Iasland). The locals who were fishermen took an instant dislike to them and their Christian beliefs and rejected the Monks idea of building a church there. The Monks feared for their lives and fled. Chastened and disgusted the Monks cast three curses on the valley. Nant's ground would never be consecrated again was the first. This meant that no-one could be buried there. Members of the same family would not be allowed to marry each other, the second one. The final one indicated that Nant would succeed and fail three times before failing forever.

There are three quarries associated with Nant Gwrtheyrn:

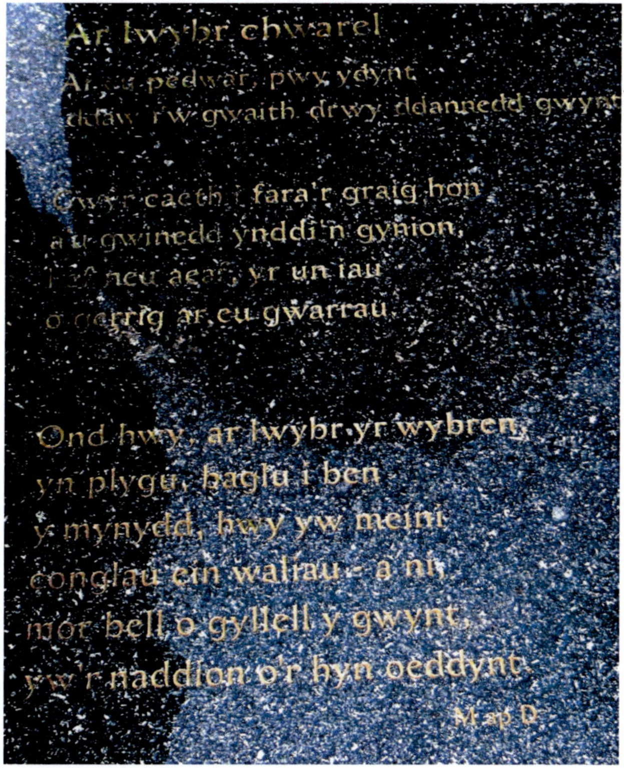

The poem at the sculpture to the memorial to the quarrymen of Nant Gwrtheyrn in the car park before the road descends

Cae'r Nant

Map: Ordnance Survey 1:25,000 Lleyn Peninsula East/Pen Llŷn Ardal Ddwyreiniol Grid reference: SH 354 453

Sometimes referred to as Trwyn y Gorlech. Cae'r Nant was operational between 1859 and 1939 although low key extraction took place between 1946 and 1951. As with the other quarries in the area they became part of the Welsh Granite Co. Ltd, owned by Kneeshaw and Lupton after they bought them in 1861.The impressive incline, long since degraded, was some 2,700 feet (820 metres) long which connected the quarry to the iron and timber jetty. There are remains of winding houses, barracks and crushing plant. Not only were ships loaded with setts from the jetty below this quarry the other two quarries in the area, Porth y Nant and Carreg y Llam also shipped theirs from their own jetties on a regular basis.

It is worth mentioning here that when descending Garn Ganol towards Bwlch yr Eifl there are a number of curious stacked stones forming bays. These are seen to the left of the path and is the site, perhaps, of an ancient stone quarry or collection point.

1. Looking across to the stone crusher at Cae'r Nant from the road descending to Nant Gwrtheyrn;
2. Looking across to Cae'r Nant, Nant Gwrtheyrn and Porth y Nant from the top of Carreg y Llam;
3. The largest of the Pistyll stone quarries seen when walking from Pistyll to Penrhyn Glas headland and Carreg y Llam;
4. Cae'r Nant seen across the other side of the valley from close to the powder house above Porth y Nant;
5. Looking down to Nant Gwrtheyrn from the track leading to Bwlch yr Eifl;
6. Carreg y Llam and Nant Gwrtheyrn seen from the track leading down to Cae'r Nant with ruins to the right

1

4

2

5

3

6

1. Cae'r Nant barracks ruin. The walled area to the right was possibly a small garden?;
2. Blacksmiths ruin on the upper level;
3. Derelict incline and wall;
4. Ruined cabin with the Nant Gwrtheyrn cascading down the impressive cliff;
5. Drum house to the left and barracks

1. Drum house;
2. Drum house and barracks;
3. General view of the quarry infrastructure as viewed from the track leading to Bwlch yr Eifl;
4. Cae'r Nant quarry towering above the hopper by the beach;
5. Stacked stone on the west side of Garn

Porth y Nant

Map: Ordnance Survey 1:25,000 Lleyn Peninsula West/Pen Llŷn Ardal Orllewinol Grid reference: SH 347 445

As with other quarries in the area this too was bought by the Liverpool based Kneeshaw and Lupton in 1861 to form the Welsh Granite Co. Ltd. At their peak the three Nant Gwrtheyrn quarries employed 110 men. The main output was rectangular setts carved at the quarry. The steep surrounds of the valley meant that landslides were quite common.

Workers had designated roles. '**Rock Men**' were responsible for the drilling of shot holes ready for the black powder explosive. Black powder was the ideal explosive as it had a slow burn time and produced a soft, slow blast. This had the effect of fracturing the rock to produce blocks rather than shattering it to pieces! A similar process was used in the slate quarries of Snowdonia. '**Pop Drillers**' and '**Breakers**' used hammers as well as gunpowder to break the rock that had been blasted into more manageable sizes. '**Blockers**' determined how many small sections of rock or cubes were formed from the rock. '**Settsmen**' used a dressing hammer to shape the rocks into a brick like form. Other workers such as '**Labourers**', '**Trammers**' and '**Brakemen**' brought the rock down into the crushing mill and docks.

A bit about setts here!

Setts were also made of other hard wearing rock such as gabbro or millstone grit (gritstone). Typically a sett was 4″, 6″ or 8″ square or rectangular 4″ x 6″ with a thickness of around 2″ to 3″. Making setts was a great skill entailing a three to four years long 'apprenticeship' to learn the techniques involved. '**Settmen**' would stand and used several types of hammer:

SCABBLER – This was used for breaking the crust of the rock which could then be termed Scabbled as it was now roughly dressed but showed prominent tool marks. The act of Scabbling was a process of removing surface irregularities for blocks to be stored or for shipment, whereas Scabblings were small chips of stone.

MOLI MAWR or SLEDGE – This was the heaviest one of all and weighed in at 40 pounds!

'HAMMER WITHOUT A HANDLE' – Weighed in at 10 pounds. It was sharpened at one end and used on larger rocks.
'DOUBLED HANDED HAMMER' – Was used to create a hole by hand by turning the borer and the other for striking the stone.
MEIDRYDD or IRON GAUGE – Used for accurate measurements of setts.
Nowadays setts are roughly rectangular with a depth and width between 3″ to 8″ (75 to 200mm) and a length of 3″ to 18″ (75 to 450mm).

1. The office ruin;
2. Stone crusher;
3. Storage hopper;
4. Remains of the pier abutment at Porth y Nant, Nant Gwrtheyrn

High above Nant Gwrtheyrn, almost at the edge of the quarry, is a fine Powder House also known as a Magazine. Each quarry had its own, possibly, even, having two. Inside these black powder was kept for blasting. Being volatile stuff the 'houses' were built well away from the quarries as it had a habit of just going off, randomly. Being built to satisfy safety requirements these buildings would have been lined with wood to keep the powder dry. The roof of this house is very fine indeed. It is vaulted and built from the setts made in the quarry.

When the setts were ready for shipment wood trucks ran down narrow railway lines to the jetty whilst the empty ones went back up to be filled again. From there conveyor belts loaded with rock ran along the jetty to be loaded directly onto the waiting boats. The quarry closed in 1939 but was subsequently bought by the Amalgamated Roadstone Corporation Ltd.

1. The powder house high above Porth y Nant with Nant Gwrtheyrn seen down to the right;
2. General view of the upper quarry at Porth y Nant, Nant Gwrtheyrn;
3. Looking down on to the stone crusher;
4. A 'paved' incline bed;
5. A drum house and shelter in the upper quarry;
6.Nant Gwrtheyrn and Porth y Nant stone quarry as seen from Carreg y Llam;
7. The powder house high above Porth y Nant with Nant Gwrtheyrn to the left;
8. Looking across to the stone crusher and hopper with Cae'r Nant in the background to the left and Garn Fôr to the right

6

7

5

8

1

4

2

5

3

6

1. Geared wheel among the ruins;
2. Rusting machinery in the ruins;
3. A rusted lathe with the manufacturers name;
4. The office when seen from the rear;
5. A hopper high up the hillside;
6. Looking down to the main ruined buildings with the pier abutment;
7. Ruined, rusted cart;
8. The rusted lathe in the mine buildings;
9. A view of Carreg y Llam from the buildings with the lathe;
10. Remains of the drum house drum below Porth y Nant quarry

Carreg y Llam

Map: Ordnance Survey 1:25,000 Lleyn Peninsula West/Pen Llŷn Ardal Orllewinol
Grid reference: SH 335 43

The quarry was also known as Penrhyn Glas. Carreg y Llam cliff is important for nesting seabirds such as guillemots and kittiwakes in spring. The quarry commenced work in 1908 by H. J. Wright. He had previously operated the Trefor quarry and had a long track record in slate, manganese, iron and gold mining in North Wales. He employed between 40 and 60 workers between 1911 – 14. During World War I the workforce dwindled to 2. Revival came in 1920 when the London based Carreg y Llam Ltd took over and became National Road Materials. A new pier was built between 1920 and 1927 and at that time 45 to 70 men worked there plus other outworkers. In 1934 it became part of Amalgamated Roadstone.

There were various advantages over Porth y Nant as there was road access, of sorts, and much deeper water for ships to dock. In fact there were two wharves here. One of these had fixed chutes that were fed, initially by tramway tubs, via a conveyor. This was capable of loading 100 tons in 15 minutes!

The company operated the steamships *Maggie Purves* and *Panmure*. In the late 1920's electric stone crushers were installed for the production of macadam, railway ballast and aggregates. Carreg y Llam during World War II operated until closure in November 1963.

In 1950 the company sold out to Amalgamated Roadstone Corporation Ltd who had also acquired the Porth y Nant quarry. Carreg y Llam provided jobs for Nefyn workers long after work had ceased at the ones around Nefyn.

Small scale quarries can be seen when approaching Carreg y Llam from Pistyll. The largest of these is at the end nearest to Pistyll.

1. Carreg y Llam as seen from the coastal path; 2. The largest of the Pistyll stone quarries seen when walking from Pistyll to Penrhyn Glas headland and Carreg y Llam; 3. Carreg y Llam stone quarry on Penrhyn Glas, taken from the coastal path near the start of the walk from Nant Gwrtheyrn

3

Moel Tŷ Mawr/Bodeilas

Map: Ordnance Survey 1:25,000 Lleyn Peninsula West/Pen Llŷn Ardal Orllewinol
Grid reference: SH 319 421

The quarry was established by Herbert Thomas of Tŷ Mawr, Pistyll. It was situated on the headland of Penrhyn Bodeilas. In 1861 it was leased to Richard Morris Griffith, a banker: Hedworth Lee, a civil engineer and William Darbishire a slate owner. They formed the Tŷ Mawr Granite Company in 1863 amalgamating with the Welsh Granite Company along with others in the area in 1864. The quarry was sold in 1866 and successive companies took control over the following years. In 1901 some 84 workers were employed but it closed in 1907. Their setts were exported via Doc Bodeilas.

Looking down to the pier on Penrhyn Bodeilas

Stone Quarries associated with Nefyn

Nefyn, perhaps, is more noted for its fishing. Indeed the town's coat of arms incorporates three herrings. However, very close to the village are several quarries. There are Gwylwyr and the nearby Tŷ Mawr/Bodeilas. On Mynydd Nefyn two quarries close together are Moel Dywyrch and John Lloyd. Whilst not producing the amount of stone the ones centred on Nant Gwrtheyrn and Trefor they were still reasonably large undertakings. Rounded sea washed stones were used to pave the streets of Nefyn and were also exported to places such as Liverpool. These stones were called cobbles proving unsuitable for horse drawn wagons and were replaced by rectangular setts as they provided a much flatter surface.

A census in 1851 noted that of the population of Nefyn there were 58 quarry workers in the area of which 9 of these were quarrymen, 9 as sett makers, 33 as stone cutters plus another 7 identified as being apprentices.

Gwylwyr

Map: Ordnance Survey 1:25,000 Lleyn Peninsula West/Pen Llŷn Ardal Orllewinol
Grid reference: SH 319 414

Gwylwyr was the main stone quarry around Nefyn and had started production in 1835. Samuel Holland a pioneer in the slate industry bought the Nefyn and Trefor quarries in 1844. His foreman was Trevor Jones whose name was given for the village of Trefor. In order for Holland to concentrated on his slate business he sold the quarry to Messrs Hutton and Roscoe. As the demand for stone increased more people came to the area. Many seemed to favour Pistyll less than a mile away from Gwylwyr. By 1900 over 100 men worked in Gwylwyr. Demand for setts went into decline at the start of World War I and by 1937 only two men were employed. The jetty at Wern was blown up during World War II to prevent it being used by enemy ships.

Interestingly it is purported that 60,000 setts had been produced from the Trefor and Nefyn quarries between 1850 and 1864. In Manchester alone 44 main streets had been paved with these setts.

The outbreak of World War I virtually closed Gwylwyr but in 1913–14 there were still more than 60 workers employed. There was no production between 1916 and 1920. The 1920's and 30's saw little production but the quarry was still being worked and by 1937 there were only two men employed when production ceased.

1

2

The prominent incline ran from the quarry across the road and on to a jetty at Wern. Ships frequently came and setts loaded for shipment to Liverpool. These ships were owned by the quarry owner.

As with the other stone quarries on Gyrn Ddu the only activity seen here nowadays are infrequent visits by rock climbers for a very out of the way experience.

1. General view of Gwylwyr and its stone quarry;
2. Approaching Gwylwyr stone quarry;
3. Gwylwyr and the stone quarry showing the fine incline;
4. Looking up the upper section of the main incline from the footpath below

1. The side wall of the incline;
2. Rusted dram;
3. The very degraded upper incline above the first level;
4. The drum house on the first level;
5. The quarry floor on the first level;
6. Looking down the main section of incline from the first level;
7. The substantial spoil heaps below the first level;
8. The drum house at the top of the upper incline showing the degraded incline wall

1

2

3

1. The drum house at the top of the upper incline. Porthdinllaen can be seen between the walls;
2. Looking down to the drum house on the lower level;
3. The drum house on the uppermost level;
4. & 5. Revetment below a spoil heap on the upper level;
6. Looking across to Garn Fadryn from the upper spoil heap revetment. John Lloyd quarry can be seen just to the left of the spoil heap left of centre

5

4

6

Other Quarries close to Gwylwyr

These quarries opened some time later with **MOEL TŶ GWYN** SH 329 415 in 1864 and known as the Vaynol and Nanhoron Quarries in the parish of Pistyll. **FOEL DYWYRCH** SH 324 407 close to the summit of Mynydd Nefyn opened in 1881. The Nefyn United Granite Quarries acquired this site in 1886 but it was never successful and closed rather suddenly in 1903.

JOHN LLOYD SH 314 407. This small quarry low down on Mynydd Nefyn opened in 1866. It too closed in the early 20th century although it was spasmodically worked until 1937. With Gwylwyr quarry being partially successful John Lloyd Jones from Nantlle and his business partner John Hughes of Manchester took a 21 years lease of some land in 1866 on Mynydd Nefyn that belonged to Lord Newborough having realised that profit could be made from quarrying granite. In 1868 it was recorded that the quarry was operational but subsequently lay idle until 1921 when it was re-opened by Henry Griffith as the **ARVONIA QUARRY**. The quarry was in a poor position with difficult access Thirty two men were employed in 1925. By 1931 the number of men working had shrunk to 10. In 1934 only 9 worked there and these were only employed part time or as seasonal workers. However, the most profit was made by a larger than life character called Wil Blore. Wil was a tall man with a craggy appearance who had a very loud and brash voice. He made his living by hauling the quarried material down the hillside by horse and cart until the quarry closed in 1937.

1. Tŷ Gwyn stone quarry;
2. Ruined quarry building at Foel Dywyrch and view towards Carreglefain;
3. The lower ruins at Foel Dywyrch and view towards Carreglefain;
4. Looking up to Foel Dywyrch quarry with the ruins below;
5. John Lloyd quarry from below;
6. The tramway wall;
7. Gwylwyr from the top of John Lloyd

Carreg Imbill

Map: Ordnance Survey 1:25,000 Lleyn Peninsula West/Pen Llŷn Ardal Orllewinol Grid reference: SH 286 342

Also known as Gimlet Rock. Many years ago Carreg y Imbill was an island but over time sand dunes built up to the west of it and formed not only Pwllheli Beach but, also, Abererch Beach to the east. The quarry was quite a large affair and had commenced operating in the 1850's by the Liverpool and Pwllheli Granite Co Ltd. In the 1890's quarrying was being done by Brundritt & Co of Runcorn. Work ceased in the interwar years after much of the crag had been quarried away! The remains are now a caravan park and sailing club. Setts were exported from the pier in Pwllheli to far off places such as Canada and the United States on ships that had brought in timber. There was a crane on the quayside for loading ships. Very quickly there were 150 workers there. Just like other areas of Llŷn, people came from all over Wales and beyond. Many had quarry working skills. Work continued spasmodically with times of output and inactivity. A strike in the 1880's occurred when the owners wanted to lower wages. As a result many of the workers moved on, some to Ireland and some to Scotland.

The greatest time of output were the years prior to the World War I when over 170 were employed. During the religious revival of 1904 to 1905 the quarry closed for four hours to enable workers to go to a prayer meeting. Setts destined for use in England were, initially, taken by ship but during the 1920's and 30's lorries were carrying smaller stone from the quarry. Final closure came in 1939 when the lease was not renewed as the rock had been reduced substantially. A fine feature below the rock is a tidal inlet where water swirls ominously at high tide. It is called Crochan Berw which translates very aptly to the boiling cauldron! It is also a favoured spot for anglers and also for people learning to rock climb.

Pwllheli is regarded as the capital of Llŷn. A small town with many facilities. The name translates in English to 'salt water pool'. It was granted a charter in 1355 by Edward, the Black Prince (15 June 1330 – 8th June 1376), otherwise known as Edward of Woodstock. He was the eldest son of Edward III. Not only was he a fine military leader Edward was the only English Prince of Wales never to rule as king dying a year before his father. Edward's son came to the throne as a minor and became Richard II. A Wednesday market is held year round in the centre of the town. Shipbuilding and fishing were the predominant industries as well as a small stone quarry at Gimlet Rock (Carreg yr Imbill), but tourism has now taken over. The railway arrived in 1867. Plaid Cymru, the Welsh Parliamentary party, was founded here in 1925.

1. The landward side of Carreg Imbill rock tower;
2. The seaward face of Carreg Imbill

Mynydd Tir y Cwmwd (Tan y Mynydd)

Map: Ordnance Survey 1:25,000 Lleyn Peninsula West/Pen Llŷn Ardal Orllewinol
Grid reference: Quarry 2 SH 329 304

There are five disused quarries above the beach before reaching the headland of Trwyn Llambedrog. They are sometimes referred to as Ty'n Tywyn and can be approached with care from a car parking area at the end of the tarmac road below quarry 2. Quarry three can be reached by walking along the sandy beach at LOW TIDE. The industry lasted almost a century providing work for the men of Llanbedrog but closing finally in 1949. Setts and chippings were produced. The obvious and main remains are: Four support timbers of the old jetty, a fine incline wall with a curious small rectangular shaped hole part way up at the base of the incline and a fine concrete hopper further along.

Although nothing to do with these quarries is an 'iron man' close to the summit of Mynydd Tir y Cwmwd. This is well worth the visit when in the area for the terrific views to be had over the bay and to the distant peaks of Snowdonia. There have been three 'Iron Men' here, although the original was constructed from wood. It was a figurehead from a ship and erected in 1919 on the headland by the

1

2

family of Solomon Andrews (1835–1908) a wealthy Cardiff business man. He was also the owner of Plas Glyn y Weddw. Unhappily the wood figure was burnt by vandals and the villagers decided to erect another. Simon van de Put a local artist/sculptor who lived in Llanbedrog from 1976–1990 was contacted to see if he could construct a figure to replace the one burnt. It was constructed from recycled steel sheet and bar. This 'Iron Man' was erected in March 1980. Simon donated his time to the construction and only charged £50 for the materials used. Unfortunately, as the metal was untreated it quickly fell into decay and the man literally fell out of his boots! A refurbishment took place in 1987. This was paid for by a summer resident from Lytham St. Anne's in Lancashire. When this finally fell apart a replacement was brought in by helicopter and set into position over the Jubilee weekend on June 1st 2002. This new one was designed and built by local village talent. It included Berwyn Jones the designer and two craftsmen Davis and Hugh Jones. On a windy day the 'Iron Man' sings!

Llanbedrog itself is also well worth visiting. The village derives its name from the establishment of the church by St. Pedrog in the 6th century. Note that for the village name the p is mutated to b!

1. Quarry 2; 2. Quarry 2 seen from the beach; 3. The incline wall leading down to the beach from the upper quarries; 4. Ruined works buildings

3

4

Legend tells us that Pedrog was a prince who gave up inheriting his father's kingdom and became a monk in Bodmin, Cornwall becoming one of the chief saints of Somerset, Devon and Cornwall as well as Brittany. He is also a patron saint of two other Welsh churches one in Pembrokeshire, St Petrox and another close to Cardigan at Ferwig.

The church suffered greatly at the hands of Cromwell's troops in the Civil War. The church walls were destroyed as were the ancient east window and several gravestones. Geoffrey Parry who led the army used the church to stable his horses. He was an ardent Puritan who, oddly, married the heiress of Wern Fawr in 1642. This family were staunch Royalists. They had a son called Love God Parry. In 1693 Love Parry, he rarely used his middle name, set about righting his father's wrongs to restore the church. The Love Parry family later established themselves at Madryn although they were all buried in the family vault at Llanbedrog.

The building of Plas Glyn y Weddw started in 1856 and completed in 1857 as a Dower house for Lady Elizabeth Love Jones Parry of the Madryn Estate after the death of her husband in 1853. She had a large art collection and the house was designed to house this collection by the architect Henry Kennedy. The cost of the building to include all the furniture, the fine gardens that included some quite exotic species of trees and plants as well as creating a network of paths through the Winllan grounds was £20,000. Lady Love

1. The remains of the jetty;
2. Mynydd Tir y Cwmwd from Machroes

had intended to live in the house when Thomas, her son, married. He didn't do so until after his mother's death. In actuality she never spent a single night there although she was a frequent daytime visitor.

One of the reasons why the house was built there was that Lady Love's husband, Sir Love Jones-Parry was buried with his ancestors in the cemetery at Llanbedrog church which is very close to the house. Lady Love wanted to live near his grave and a special path was created to the churchyard. Another reason was that Elizabeth Caldecott, who became Elizabeth Jones-Parry following her marriage to the squire of Madryn, had been raised at the Cottage, a villa owned by the Madryn family near the church in Llanbedrog.

In 1896, Plas Glyn y Weddw came up for sale. Solomon Andrews, the wealthy Cardiff business man mentioned above, bought the house for £7,000. This gave him the golden opportunity to further his business developments along the Peninsula. He turned the building into a public art gallery where he exhibited paintings by famous artists such as Gainsborough and Turner. Today there is a very fine tea room and the gallery still has exhibitions. These change throughout the year.

1. The huge concrete hopper;
2. Walling below the internal tramway

Trwyn Dwmi (Porth y Pistyll)

Map: Ordnance Survey 1:25,000 Lleyn Peninsula West/Pen Llŷn Ardal Orllewinol
Grid reference: SH 163 251

The most striking feature here is the obvious stone harbour wall. This is seen from the coastal path easily followed south from Aberdaron. Work commenced here in 1901 when it was managed by Hugh Evans. Setts were made and eight houses started to be built at Bodermid Isaf but remained unfinished. The foundations of six were laid but only two completed and can be still be seen today from the minor road that passes close to them. The quarry was a very difficult place to work. Ladders had to be placed to make access easier for the workers. In 1904/05 Evans erected a timber and stone jetty at Porth y Pistyll. This was quite an elaborate affair including a steam crane for loading the setts onto the ships. The setts were 4, 6 and 8 inches (100, 150 and 200 mms). Kerb stones were also made. In 1908 another quarry opened up nearby, Craig y Cwlwm. The harbour wall and jetty was too low, often ravaged by the sea making it costly to maintain. In 1907 the Co-operative Granite Quarries Ltd was registered with Charles Sheridan Jones as the managing director along with three others. Workers would get a share of the profits which was on top of their wages. Being in a relatively remote position it was difficult to attract workers so in 1908 the company created another, The Aberdaron Co-operative Housing Society. An architect, Harold Lander, a pioneer of the Garden City Movement, was employed to draw up plans for a village. His, somewhat fanciful, proposal was to have 91 cottages along a tree lined street on the nearby farmland. This would also have shops and a reading room overlooking a village green.

Another subsidiary, the Coal Consumers' Pioneer Society, proposed to supply the residents of Aberdaron with coal. This would be sold to them cheaply

1. The harbour at Porth y Pistyll; 2. Looking down into Porth y Pistyll with the harbour wall to the right; 3. Remains of the harbour below Trwyn Dwmi stone quarry when viewed from the south

3

as it would come directly from a re-opened colliery at Mold. This would cut out the middleman. In 1909 Charles became bankrupt after losing a libel case. He had sunk all his money into these schemes and the companies were wound up in 1915.

In 1930 the quarries and harbour were re-opened by Frank Jackson. He set about improving the facilities when some 45 men worked at the quarry. However, it was closed by 1937 and never re-opened again. No setts were sold during this period! In 1940 it was said there were 600 setts and a cartload of kerbstones just left on site. It is rumoured that several houses used the setts for fireplaces in the village!

Aberdaron is a small but pretty village and well worth visiting. It is a former fishing village and often referred to as 'The Land's End of Wales', is very picturesque. It was the last stop for pilgrims on their way to Ynys Enlli. Industry had its place here at one time with quarrying in the area (for limestone, lead, jasper and manganese) and shipbuilding taking place. Now, however, it is the tourist industry that has taken over due to the fine beach and a number of good amenities. It is possible that people have lived here for over 2,500 years. There are two bridges in the village. One, Pont Fach, over the often dry Afon Cyll-y-Felin was one of two built

Bodermid Isaf

in 1823. The other, Pont Fawr, spans the Afon Daron. The coast around here has been the site of many ship wrecks. Aberdaron is renowned for its pure air having very low levels of air pollution. As such rare lichens grow such as the golden hair. This has a very low tolerance to air pollution and frosts are rare. The church of St. Hywyn is dedicated to Hywyn the son of King Arthur's sister Gwenonwy and her husband Gwyndaf Hen. There was most likely a wooden building here that was replaced by a stone building around 1100. An extension to the church was added around 1500 to accommodate the influx of pilgrims. Y Gegin Fawr a café in the village is a 17th century building that housed the pilgrims prior to their voyage across the treacherous Swnt Enlli (Bardsey Sound).

Bodermid Isaf

Before leaving the stone section mention must be made of brick manufacturing at Morfa Nefyn, Porth Neigwl and Pwllheli. Whilst not in essence occurring naturally, it was made from local natural material. The brickworks at Morfa at Morfa Nefyn SH 2818 4072 operated from 1868 to 1906. It was run by Captain David Hughes, Shop Groefford and John Roberts. A tall chimney was a prominent feature whilst the wooden jetty below the site was built to transport the finished product by sea. The site is now a National Trust car park.

There were two more sites producing bricks. One was Porth Neigwl SH 2584 2821 operating between 1890 and 1900 when it was marked as disused on the OS map. On 29th July 1898 John Hunter, a partner in 'Hunter and Howells's Brickworks, Porth Neigwl' was sued for bankruptcy claiming it was his inability to sell the bricks due to the actions of one of his creditors.

The other one was, apparently, situated near to Bryn Hynnog, close to Pwllheli at SH 3654 3657. No evidence has been found but supposedly operated between 1899 and 1938. It was the second attempt by Messrs Hunter and Howell after their failed venture at Port Neigwl.

Section 2 – Manganese Mines

Overview

The two main areas where manganese was mined are centred around Rhiw. It is a brittle, silvery metal, a chemical element with the symbol Mn. It's atomic number is 25. The uses of manganese are diverse. It was used in the manufacture of bleach; the steel industry; glass making and in the metallurgical and chemical industries. Manganese was mainly used to create stronger steel, especially stainless. Beginning in the mid 19th century it was used extensively to increase the wear resistance and hardness of steel. This is the largest use today with some 90% of the world production of manganese being used in the iron and steel industries. Around 8 to 14lbs (4 to 6Kgs) of manganese are used in every ton of steel depending on the product. Welsh ores were found to be of low quality. As such their main value was as a direct additive to the blast furnace.

Manganese oxide is used as an oxidising agent, as a rubber additive, in glass making, fertilisers and ceramics. Manganese sulphate can be used as a fungicide. Not only is it an essential dietary requirement important in macronutrient metabolism, bone formation and free radical defence systems it is a critical component in dozens of proteins and enzymes. Interestingly aluminium drink cans contain about 1.5 percent manganese.

Rhiw has existed for many centuries. On the side of Mynydd y Graig to the south of the village are three hill forts several hut circles and remnants of terraced fields which are thought to date back to the late Iron Age. On the side of Mynydd Rhiw is a late Stone Age burial chamber as well as Neolithic stone quarries although these are barely visible today The Common Land here was enclosed by an Act of Parliament in 1811. Barley and Oats were grown. When Manganese was discovered in 1827 donkeys were, initially, used to transport the ore to Porth Cadlan and Porth Neigwl. In the late 19th century the village grew when houses were built for the quarry workers. By 1914 an aerial ropeway had been constructed. This passed over the village from the Rhiw/Benallt mines to the jetty at Porth Neigwl. During World War I a huge demand arose for manganese. This provided much work for the people in the village. Around 200 people were employed in 1906. During World War II coal miners, Cornish tin miners, along with a contingent of the Royal Canadian Engineers, came to work in the mines. In total some 15,000 tons of ore were extracted during the lifetime of these mines.

Nant Gadwen

Map: Ordnance Survey 1:25,000 Lleyn Peninsula West/Pen Llŷn Ardal Orllewinol
Grid reference: SH 211 266

Mining here flourished here since 1827 when the mine opened. In 1829 the recorded output was 226 tons. Initially the heavy ore was carried by donkeys to any port where a ship could berth. A pier at Porth Neigwl was not an attractive proposition. In 1902/03 a jetty was built at a cost of £182. The peak of production was in 1906 when 10,000 tons of ore were taken to Brymbo (Wrexham) along with other iron and steel centres. In its lifespan the mine produced 45,644 tons. Loaded tram road wagons took the ore down to the jetty down the steep incline their descent controlled by cables from the drum or winding house. The weight of the loaded wagons going down hauled the empty ones back up. As production increased another jetty was built. In 1918 five ships a week docked here to take ship the ore.

During the 19th century ore was carried by donkeys to Porth Cadlan to the west where it was loaded onto small boats to be taken to Ellesmere Port in Cheshire. Initially manganese was used in the production of glass and bleach. subsequently it was used to strengthen steel. Production then greatly increased. In 1903 the British Manganese Company and the North Wales Manganese Company opened adjoining mines.

The on site railway lines, were inexplicably, of different gauges but the main one was 2 feet (610 mms). However, the incline used a 3 feet (305 mms) gauge. It is known that at least one steam purpose built locomotive 0-4-0 saddle tank worked here and also operated from Benallt mine. It was named appropriately Rhiw and built by Bagnalls of Stafford. Production declined after the World War I as the ore

1. Spoil heaps at the lower end of Nant Gadwen with the island of Maen Gwenonwy beyond to the right. The island was supposedly named after King Arthur's sister; 2. Looking down Nant Gadwen; 3. One of the adits leading into the Nant Gadwen manganese mine; 4. The ruined weighbridge building and drum house at the top of the incline leading down to the jetty in Porth Ysgo

1

2

3

4

was not of the highest quality, Superior foreign ores could be sourced and bought by the mine's customers. The mine closed on Monday 17th August 1925. The Porth Ysgo jetty was last used in 1927 and demolished in 1933.

1. Porth Ysgo. The incline leading down to the jetty ran down the slope in front of the rocky promontory;
2. Looking up the tramway;
3. The uppermost drum house and drum skeleton;
4. An entrance, although short, on the true right of Nant Gadwen;
5. The view out of an entrance on the true right of Nant Gadwen

1. Another entrance into the mine on the true right of Nant Gadwen;
2. Looking out of a major entrance on the true left of Nant Gadwen;
3. The wall rising from the Nant Gadwen that supported the railway line to the incline leading down to the jetty on Porth Ysgo;
4. An entrance into the Nant Gadwen manganese mines high above the valley

Rhiw/Benallt

Map: Ordnance Survey 1:25,000 Lleyn Peninsula West/Pen Llŷn Ardal Orllewinol Grid reference: SH 222 281

Benallt mine started out quite late, only opening in 1886. Work was abandoned in 1894. Rhiw and Benallt were separately owned but they worked the same seam of ore. Both their underground and surface workings amalgamated. The north eastern part of the workings were worked by the Rhiw Mine were on Crown land whilst the larger Benallt Mine to the south west was in private ownership. It is unclear where the boundary was. However, the large rusted steam boiler that is seen there is on the site of Rhiw.

Benallt Mine started being re-worked again in 1904 and became known as Benallt no 2 Mine after further veins were found. By 1914, however, the ore appears to have been exhausted and the company started to develop the Nant Gadwen mine a mile or so to the south, south west and continued until 1925 when production ceased.

Once again Benallt was re-opened this time by the Ministry of Defence in 1939 to produce minerals for the war effort. This incorporated Rhiw Mine.

1. The remains of the aerial ropeway;
2. The rusted remains of the steam boiler;
3. One of the shafts with shelters below and beyond;
4. Spoil heap and pit;
5. Quarry building ruins;
6. The heavily rusted drum at the head of the incline that lead down to Porth Ysgo

2

3

4

5

6

Section 3 – Lead/Copper Mines

Overview

Some say that lead was first mined in the area by the Romans. However, this seems doubtful as there is very little evidence of this. The earliest recorded mining was in 1638 by Thomas Bushell. He sought to mine silver for the new royal mint that had been set up in Aberystwyth Castle. The venture was very short lived. Subsequent attempts at mining were also very short lived, unsuccessful and of a sporadic nature. Penrhyn Du was the without doubt the first mine to open for its lead and silver. Production continued for the next 250 years albeit, as mentioned above, sporadically. Copper was found in Pantgwyn but in the early days it was not found to be of sufficient quantity to be commercial until around 1869. However, production ceased in 1892.

One owner it is reputed to have paid his workers in potatoes! At least they and their families had food. Other owners thought that recruiting miners from the tin mines of Cornwall would solve the problem. Alas not. Cornish Row cottages remain close to the Engine House but are on private land. Pumping water from the mines was very expensive and markets uncertain.

The jetty on Penrhyn Du was built for ships to dock and for the shipment of ore and to unload commodities. A tramline built in 1842, passed over the main portal to the mine, ran from the headland to Llanengan at a time when Penrhyn Du was the only mine in the area. Some of it remains and is used as an access track from Machroes to the headland and the old lifeboat station, now part of a finely situated house. Wagons along the line were horse drawn. Some mine buildings of Penrhyn Du have been incorporated into the Porth Tocyn Hotel. Other mines subsequently opened that linked into this, notably Pantgwyn, Tan y Bwlch and Daugoch.

The line was originally built to transport the iron ore being found close to Llanengan, although the amount of ore being produced was minute. Mining had begun in 1836 in Tanyrafon, Creigir and close to the Pen y Gaer hill fort. As mines closed the line was abandoned in 1885/86.

The main mines of the area were –

- Penrhyn Du
- Tan y Bwlch – part of Penrhyn Du
- West Assheton – a part of Penrhyn Du
- Port Nigel (Porth Neigwl)
- Daugoch
- Pantgwyn

Penrhyn Du

Map: Ordnance Survey 1:25,000 Lleyn Peninsula West/Pen Llŷn Ardal Orllewinol Grid reference: SH 323 263 (Cornish Engine House)

Lead mining at Penrhyn Du may go back to Roman times but there is little evidence to support this. However, there were workings owned by Cymer Abbey in the Middle Ages. Mining is mentioned in 1668 as well as in 1734. In the 1760's Messrs Roe of Macclesfield in Cheshire were working the mine until the early 19th century. In 1785 John Cartwright along with three others built an engine to drain the mine. Edward Hyde Hall when he visited the area between 1809 and 1811 found that mining had ceased. In 1828 Messrs Williams of Gwennap, Cornwall, which is some 5 miles south east of Redruth, took over the running of the mine until 1839. There was a successful find in 1869 and continued to operate until 1892. In the 19th century the mine was owned by the Assheton-Smith family of Vaynol

The Penrhyn Du mines were a collection of mines. They encompassed Penrhyn Du itself, West Assheton and Tan y Bwlch. Tan y Bwlch was, most likely, the richest of them all with a recorded output of 8,722 long tons (8,862 tonnes) of lead ore. It also raised 450 long tons (460 tonnes) of zinc ore and 4,652 long tons

1

2

(4,727 tonnes) of copper ore between 1873 and 1886. NOTE: A long ton is regarded as 2,240lbs avoirdupois (1,016.05kgs), whilst a tonne is the metric form.

The most dramatic reminder of the mining hereabouts is the decayed steam powered Cornish Pump House. It is a Grade II listed building. It was built on the design of the ones found in Cornwall. The tower could well have been built in the late 18th century for a Newcomen type engine but altered in the earlt to mid 19th century to take a Boulton and Watt type beam engine. There is no visible chimney but this may have been detached. It, perhaps, is thought that Tower Cottage may well have been a separate boiler house.

Once the 19th century turned into the

1. The fine and large arched portal of the main lode just above the beach at Machroes;
2. The circular powder house easily seen from the coastal path above Penrhyn Du adjacent to the main mining area;
3. A fenced off, but run in, shaft in the main mining area;
4. The remains of the Cornish pump house

3

4

20th mining had all but ceased with a last recorded entry for 1930 as just 5 long tons. Once mining had ceased developments in the area covered the majority of the remains and little can be seen today. There is walk around the mining area starting from Machroes that starts off by following the old tramway until a rough track can be followed to a sign for the coast path. This passes the Cornish Pump House and continues to the powder house. Beyond the Engine House the fenced off flattened mining area is seen to the left. Having seen these return to the gate by the main track to follow a signed continuation of the circular walk back to Machroes.

1. The huge rampart of the pier at Penrhyn Du; 2. The remains of a ladder on the side of the pier at Penrhyn Du; 3. The jetty at Penrhyn Du; 4. Overview of Penrhyn Du lead mine with the circular powder house and Abersoch at the upper left

3

4

Port Nigel (Porth Neigwl)

Map: Ordnance Survey 1:25,000 Lleyn Peninsula West/Pen Llŷn Ardal Orllewinol
Grid reference: SH 294 267

This mine situated at Tan yr Allt, Llanengan dates back to the 17th century or earlier but closed for a long period of time. It was the most westerly one of eight in the area that mined the Main Lode that ran east to west from Penrhyn Du to Llanengan. Until 1869 the mine had been run by the North Cambrian Company. The mine was re-opened around 1869/70 when it was run by the Tan yr Allt Mining Company. They had bought it on the 14th August 1869 along with the mine buildings at Tanrallt below. It closed along with others in 1892.

Port Nigel was, possibly, the most successful of the Llanengan mines. Workings had extended to 80 fathoms (480 feet). Like many other mines in the area production was very sporadic but in 1881 it recorded a maximum of 322 tons with a total of 880 tons between 1874 and 1883. No copper or zinc was ever recorded as having been raised.

On the hillside stands a fine chimney. This is a Grade II listed structure and was built circa 1878. Its purpose is unclear whether it was used for ventilation or as a flue for abeam engine or smelter at Tanrallt below. The chimney is a

remarkable feature and can be reached easily from the village on public rights of way. At the base of the chimney is a gated fire opening. Directly below the chimney there is what appears to be a covered flue whilst in the fence slightly further down is the remains of an earlier chimney. The chimney is constructed with rubble stone to around half height then red brick banded in yellow brick with a yellow brick projecting cornice.

1. & 3. The fine chimney at Port Nigel/Tan yr Allt lead mine dominating the village high above Llanengan;
2. Looking down at the fine Port Nigel/Tan yr Allt chimney in a field with Llanengan to the right

1. Looking down at the fine Port Nigel/Tan yr Allt chimney in a field!;
2. The gated flue;
3. The remains of an earlier chimney at Port Nigel/Tan yr Allt in the fence below

Section 4 – Other Qurries – Jasper, Barytes and Coal

Mynydd Carreg Jasper Quarry

Map: Ordnance Survey 1:25,000 Lleyn Peninsula West/Pen Llŷn Ardal Orllewinol Grid reference: SH 162 292

Jasper is regarded as a semi precious stone. It is of metamorphic origin formed in the Pre-Cambrian Neoproterozoic era, a period of time between a billion and 541 million years ago. Jasper veins up to 37 metres wide were discovered on Mynydd Carreg in 1901 as well as small outcrops in the nearby sea cliffs. The discovery was, apparently, made by a group of 'gentlemen miners'. These included the mining engineer Captain John Trevethan from Rhyl. He reported that the Jasper was predominantly cherry red but some pink, buff or almost white was also in evidence.

Mining started in 1904 and continued until 1907 when a larger concern was started. Samples and chippings were sent to Birmingham. Stone experts there were amazed when they were told that there were tons of the stone available. A one ton block had been despatched to London but another block weighing in at a mighty 11 tons was despatched there in 1905. The cost of transport would have been expensive as it had to be hauled around 20 miles by traction engines to the railway station in Pwllheli. During one journey Pont Nant y Widdan, a bridge about ¾ mile from the quarry, collapsed during a haulage operation. Jasper was quite valuable. At one time a polished piece two inches square was said to command a £60 price tag at the time!

Jasper from here was regarded as being twice as strong as granite and able to withstand weathering in any climate. It was used to clad the Norwich Union building on the corner of St James Street

1. Looking up to the lookout on Mynydd Carreg; 2. Jasper bearing rock in the main quarry; 3. General view of the main quarry

1

2

3

and Piccadilly in London which opened in 1908. It was also used in Westminster Abbey and St James' Palace. Quarrying ceased quickly as the vein was exploited and had subsided substantially by 1909 but records indicate that it was still employing 18 people in 1914, the same number as in 1908. There are signs of small excavations at a farm at Llanllawen Farm (SH 146 259) but no information is known.

It is an easy walk from the Whistling Sands car park above Porth Oer along the Llŷn Coastal Path heading south to the quarry. Jasper can still be found. There is a small, free car park just above the farm at Carreg SH 164 288 by driving up the rough track to the left of the farm itself to an information board and picnic tables. Access from here is by following the track around to the left then right to reach the three small quary bays.

Shot holes

opposite: The remains of the water powered mill

Gwaith y Pompren Barytes Mine

Map: Ordnance Survey 1:25,000 Lleyn Peninsula West/Pen Llŷn Ardal Orllewinol
Grid reference: SH 167 264

Barytes is also known as heavy spar, a barium sulphate. It is an insoluble mineral used mainly today as an agent to increase weight in drilling for oil and gas. In its purest white form it is used as a filler in paints, paper and ceramics.

The Gwaith y Pompren mine workings at Porth Simdde, east of the Afon Saint, to the west of Aberdaron were worked between 1905 and 1913 and again very briefly in 1918. However, it is thought that it was mined much earlier, around 1837 and was of good quality. The maximum number of men working here never numbered more than four. Once mined the barytes was, initially, loaded onto ships on the beach.

In 1905 Evan J Evans, a chemist from Aberystwyth, applied to build a pier around 90 metres long. This would take the pier to below low water level. Once built it seems that it had a tramway enabling direct tipping into ships. After the mine was abandoned the pier remained intact until 1921 but was later demolished. The remnants can be seen today as forlorn stumps sticking out of the sand!

Evans owned the mine until 1911 but in 1908 he was fined £1 for storing around 18 gelignite balls in an unlocked and unregistered shed. He explained to the magistrate that he was a poor man trying to make a living and provide work for the local population and thought the fine excessive, he explained that the gelignite was harmless until connected to a detonator. Remnants of the water powered mill that ground the barytes in to a powder can be seen above high water mark.

The remains of the pier at Porth Simdde with St Tudwal's Islands on the skyline

Coal

Coal was apparently discovered, close to Pen y Groeslon and Rhoshirwaun areas in the 19th century. It was mined at Brynhunog Fawr SH 201309 in 1837 and at Rhos Cabli in 1844. It appeared that there were substantial deposits enabling a company to be formed 'The Rhoshirwaun Coal and Mining Company'. Little is known on how successful the mining was but in 1888 there was an invitation for people to invest. The mining at Rhoshirwaun SH 196 297 was in a field titled 'Cleimant' one of a number of plots behind a terrace of houses on the B4413.

Further Reading

THE LLYN PENINSULA MINES/ MWYNGLODDIO YM MHEN LLŶN by Wil Williams. Published by Gwasg Carreg Gwalch. Out of print.
ISBN: 0-86381-315-1

WALKING THE LLŶN HILLS by Des Marshall. Published by Gwasg Carreg Gwalch.
ISBN: 078-1-84524-266-4

LLŶN – Carreg Gwalch Best walks – Published by Gwasg Carreg Gwalch.
ISBN: 978-1-84524-194-0

THIS VALLEY WAS OURS by Eileen M Webb. Published by Gwasg Carreg Gwlach.
ISBN: 978-184524-255-5

NANT GWRTHEYRN by Dr Carl Clowes. Published by Ymddiriedolaeth Nant Gwrtheyrn.
ISBN: 978-0-9560072-0-9

LLŶN The Peninsula Story by Michael Senior. Published by Gwasg Carreg Gwalch.
ISBN: 1-84524-059-6

LLŶN COASTAL PATH by Des Marshall. Published by Kittiwake.
ISBN: 978 198748 43 0

METAL MINES OF LLANENGAN – Mining Ventures in a North Wales Parish by John Bennett and Robert Vernon. Published by Gwydir Nines Publications Ltd. Out of print.
ISBN: 978 095147 988 9

NEFYN – The story of an ancient Gwynedd Town and Parish by Roland Bond. Published by Gwasg Carreg Gwalch.
ISBN: 978-1-84524-124-7

QUARRYING INDUSTRY IN WALES – A HISTORY by Ian A Thomas. Published by the National Stone Centre.
IBN: 978- 1- 87182-738-5

PENMAENMAWR AND WELSH GRANITE CO LTD. A book produced as an information book by Welsh Granite Co Ltd.
No ISBN number.

MINING FOR METALS IN WALES by F. J. North. Published by the National Museum of Wales, Cardiff.
No ISBN number.

NANT GWRTHEYRN – The enchantment by Glyn Davies. Published by Glyn Davies, Photo Artist Ltd. (The book is written in Welsh and English).
ISBN: 0-955-7003-2-3

LLŶN the peninsula and its past by Ioan Roberts. Published by Gwasg Carreg Gwalch.
ISBN: 978-1-84524-243-5

TREFOR by Geraint Jones and Dafydd Williams. Published by Ganolfan Hanes Uwchgwyrfai, Clynnog Fawr, Arfon in 2006.
No ISBN number. (This book is written in Welsh).

LLŶN by Elfed Gruffydd. Adapted from the Welsh language by Gwynedd Owen. Published by Gwasg Carreg Gwalch.
ISBN: 0-86381-697-5

COMPACT CYMRU
– MORE TITLES:

www.carreg-gwalch.cymru

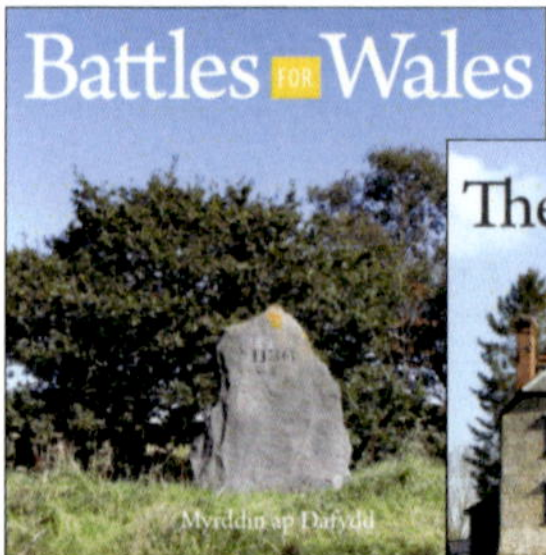

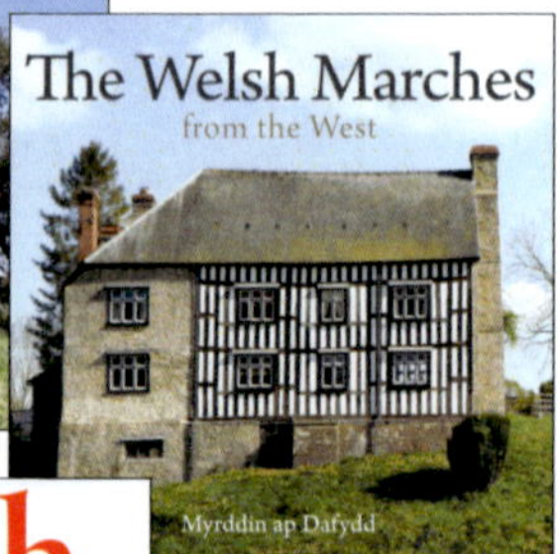

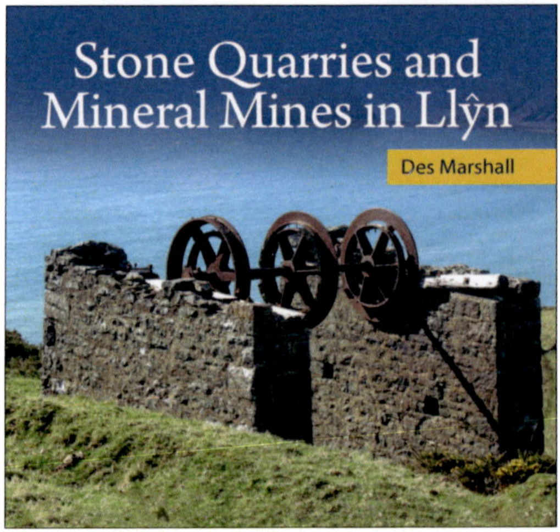

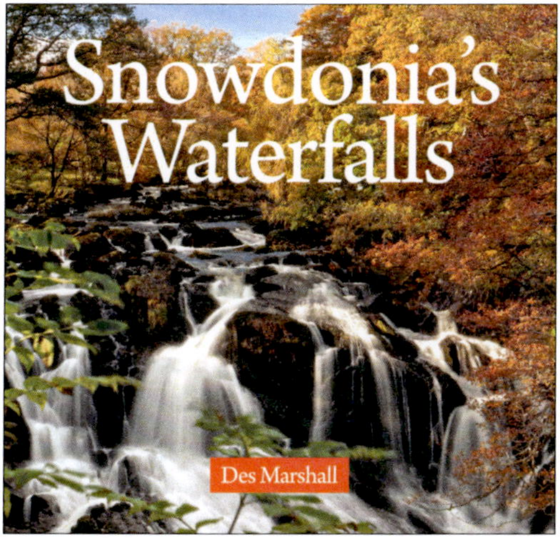
Snowdonia's
Waterfalls
Des Marshall

Day walks
FROM THE
Slate Trail of Snowdonia
Des Marshall

Jean Napier
Rhinogydd
Ancient Routes and Old Roads

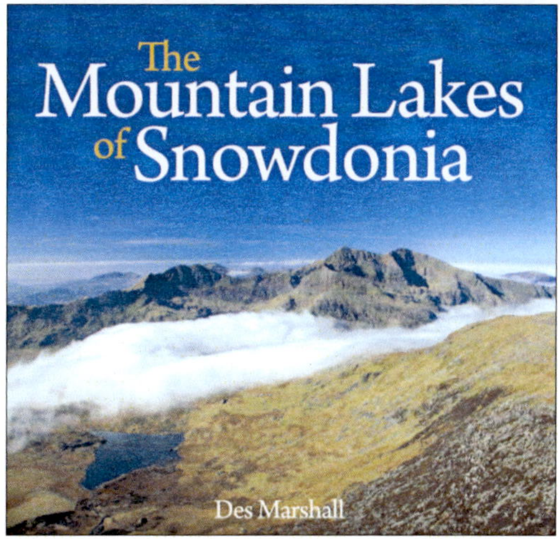
The
Mountain Lakes
of Snowdonia
Des Marshall

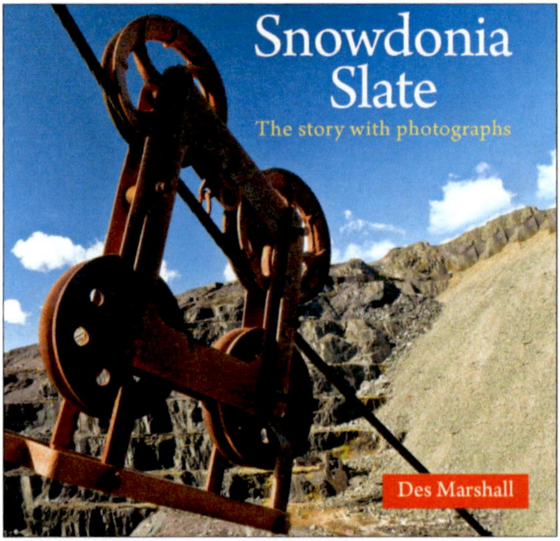
Snowdonia
Slate
The story with photographs
Des Marshall
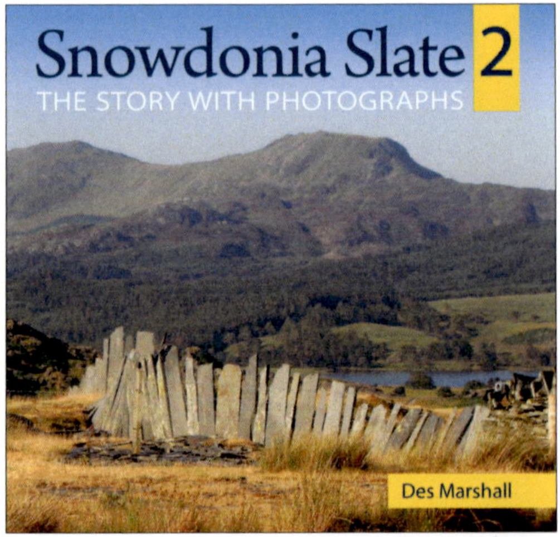
Snowdonia Slate 2
THE STORY WITH PHOTOGRAPHS
Des Marshall
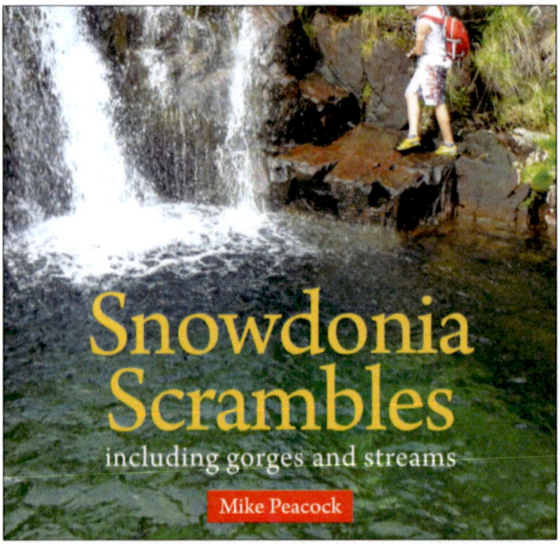
Snowdonia
Scrambles
including gorges and streams
Mike Peacock

On the Trail of the
Welsh Drovers
Twm Elias